Our
Chosen Child

A circle complete,
a child so sweet.

Our
Chosen Child

How You Came to Us
and the Growing Up Years

Conceived and Written by Judith Levy
Designed and Illustrated by Judy Pelikan

A Welcome Book

**Andrews McMeel
Publishing**

Kansas City

What Joy!
The Chosen Child

A circle complete,
A child so sweet.

A miracle baby, you!

The heart makes a cooing sound,
When a little baby's around.

So new at first,
Our whole life at last.

Oh, how sweet the smile,
From our gift of a child.

What joy to enfold,
Our baby to hold.

Sunshine, roses, rainbows too,
A miracle forever,
Our baby, you!

You had a journey to make,
A trip to come through,
To parents who were praying,
And waiting for you.

For _____

Date _____

Contents

Our Family Tree

We're two loving people,
Almost as happy as we could be,
We just needed a special angel,
To join our family tree.

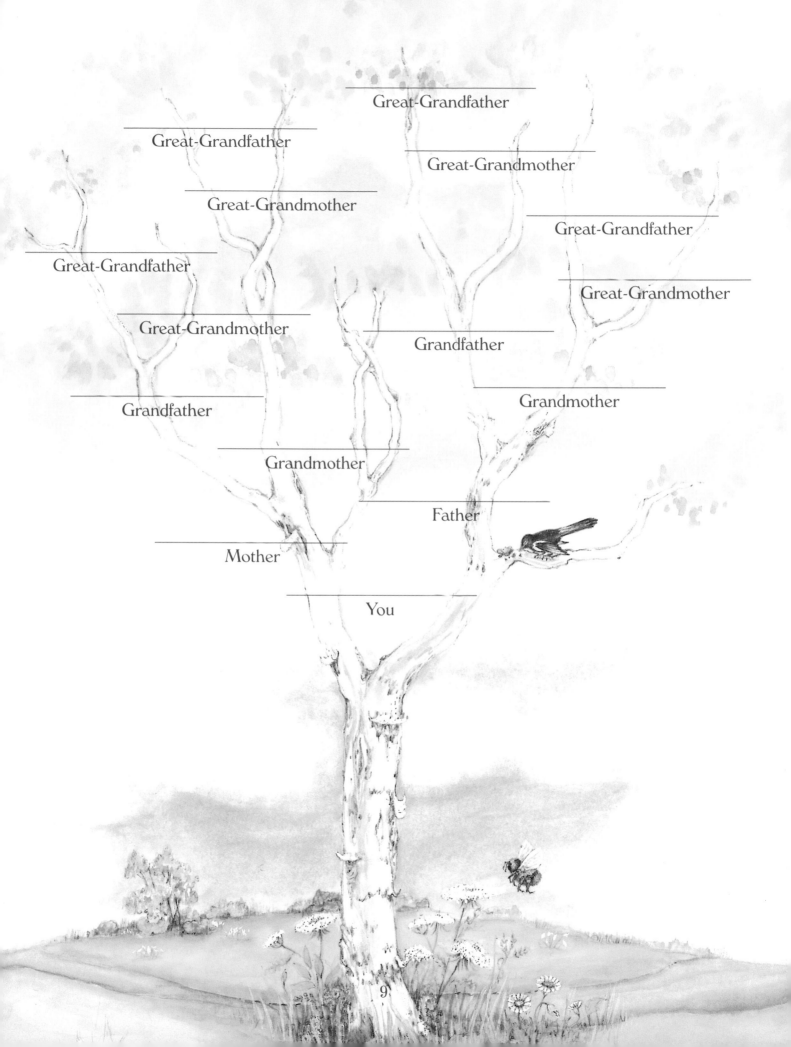

Great-Grandfather

Great-Grandfather

Great-Grandmother

Great-Grandmother

Great-Grandfather

Great-Grandfather

Great-Grandmother

Great-Grandmother

Grandfather

Grandfather

Grandmother

Grandmother

Father

Mother

You

9

Introducing Us!

Soon you'll get to know us,
We're nice as we can be.
We're Mom and Dad and with you,
We're a wonderful family.

Mom's family _____

_____

Grandparents _____

_____

Parents _____

_____

Other members of Mom's family are _____

_____

_____

_____

Dad's family _____

_____

Grandparents _____

_____

Parents _____

_____

Other members of Dad's family are _____

_____

_____

_____

All about Mom

Born _____

_____

Where _____

_____

First school attended was _____

_____

Graduated from _____

_____

Studied for _____

_____

First job was _____

_____

Now Mom's occupation is _____

_____

_____

_____

All about Dad

Born _____

_____

_____

Where _____

_____

_____

First school attended was _____

_____

_____

Graduated from _____

_____

_____

Studied for _____

_____

_____

First job was _____

_____

_____

Now Dad's occupation is _____

_____

_____

_____

How We Met

Here's the story
Of how we met,
And how we fell in love,
We'll never forget.

We met _____

_____

When _____

_____

Where _____

_____

Here's the story _____

_____

_____

We dated for _____

_____

When Dad proposed, he said _____

_____

_____

And I replied _____

_____

_____

{ PHOTO HERE }

We Were Married

Happiness was in the air,
As we stood side by side,
No one was ever more in love,
Than this bridegroom and this bride.

We were married on _____

_____

At _____

_____

We were married by _____

_____

Guests at our wedding were _____

_____

_____

_____

Special gifts we received _____

_____

_____

The most special memory of that day is _____

_____

_____

_____

Our Honeymoon

So many plans,
We were all aglow.
For a perfect honeymoon,
Here's where we decided to go.

We spent our honeymoon at _____

_____

_____

We traveled there by _____

_____

_____

We stayed there for _____

_____

_____

We had the greatest time _____

_____

_____

Our honeymoon was special because _____

_____

_____

_____

_____

Waiting for You

To fill up our hearts,
We were thinking of,
A wonderful child,
Completing our love.

When we decided to adopt a child we contacted _____

_____

Date _____

_____

At first we had to _____

_____

We were also asked to _____

_____

They wanted to know everything about us, including _____

_____

People who vouched for us were _____

_____

We had to wait till (date) _____

_____

We were so thrilled when we were told that _____

_____

_____

{ PHOTO HERE }

When We First Saw You

From the very first moment,
It was clear we knew,
The child of our dreams,
Was definitely you!

We first saw you on _____

_____

You were _____ old and we knew you were perfect for

us because _____

_____

We thought you looked _____ _____

_____

_____

What we remember most about that special day is _____

_____

_____

The first people we called were _____

_____

_____

Their reaction was _____

_____

_____

Showers of Love

Everyone was so excited,
They wanted to be there,
To share in our happiness,
Because they really care.

Your baby shower was held on _____

_____

It was given by _____

_____

Guests were _____

_____

_____

_____

Some wonderful presents were _____

_____

_____

_____

Our special memory of that day is _____

_____

_____

_____

_____

{ PHOTO HERE }

{ PHOTO HERE }

_____
NAME

_____
NAME

_____
RELATIONSHIP

_____
RELATIONSHIP

{ PHOTO HERE }

{ PHOTO HERE }

_____
NAME

_____
NAME

_____
RELATIONSHIP

_____
RELATIONSHIP

Special People Who Love You

Along with Mom and Dad,
These folks want you to know,
You're special in their lives,
And they love you so.

{ PHOTO HERE }   { PHOTO HERE }

_____   _____
NAME   NAME

_____   _____
RELATIONSHIP   RELATIONSHIP

{ PHOTO HERE }   { PHOTO HERE }

_____   _____
NAME   NAME

_____   _____
RELATIONSHIP   RELATIONSHIP

Naming Ceremony

We wanted the perfect name,
Nothing else would do,
Here's the one we chose,
And it certainly fits you.

We named you _____

_____

That name was chosen because _____

_____

You were named at _____

_____

We celebrated by _____

_____

_____

A special honor was given to _____

_____

We chose that person because _____

_____

Everyone said you looked _____

_____

It was a day of happiness because _____

_____

_____

Adoption Day

It was a magical day,
A day like no other,
For now and forever,
We'd be your father and mother.

Your adoption was made final on _____

_____

_____

Where _____

_____

_____

Judge's name _____

_____

_____

We celebrated by _____

_____

_____

What we remember most about that day is _____

_____

_____

_____

_____

{ PHOTO HERE }

Firsts

We're so amazed,
At everything you do,
From the first little smile,
And your first little coo.

The first time you slept through the night you were _____

_____

You first smiled _____

_____

You rolled over for the first time at _____ _____

_____

You sat up for the first time by yourself _____

_____

You first crawled _____

_____

Your first tooth peeked through at _____

_____

You first ate solid foods at _____

_____

Your first solid food was _____

_____

Your reaction was _____

_____

You took your first wobbly steps _____

_____

You first drank from a cup _____

_____

Your first word was _____

_____

You got your first haircut when you were _____

_____

We'll never forget the first time you _____

_____

Other important firsts _____

_____

_____

_____

_____

_____

{ PHOTO HERE }

Weekdays

From Monday to Friday,
The clock ticks away,
And here's how you spend
All your waking day.

You start your day at _____

_____

Your breakfast consists of _____

_____

Your favorite toy is _____

_____

When Mom and Dad need to be away, the person who takes care
of you is _____

_____

You will usually nap at _____

_____

For lunch you eat _____

_____

We can always get you to smile by _____

_____

Bedtime is a precious time because _____

_____

We share a special closeness when _____

_____

Weekends

During the week the hours
Slip by oh, so fast,
But on weekends we try
To make the good times last.

On Saturdays we sometimes _____
_____
_____

On Sundays we love to _____
_____
_____

Weekends we sometimes _____
_____
_____

What we like most about weekends is that _____
_____
_____

If weekends could go on, we'd love to _____
_____
_____

But it's clear that Monday we'll be ____ _____
_____
_____
_____

Traveling with You

Lots of places to see,
Lots of places to know,
We're up and we're off,
Packed and ready to go.

For our first trip we went to _____
_____
_____

We got there by _____
_____
_____

We never forgot to take along your _____
_____
_____

Your first trip on a plane was _____
_____
_____

We had such a good time when we went to _____
_____
_____
_____

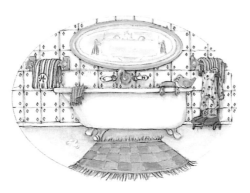

Bath Time

Splash, splash, you're having fun,
There's water everywhere.
Lots of rubs and lots of hugs,
And bubbles in the air.

You took your first bath when you were _____

_____

You had your bath in _____

_____

Your reaction was _____

_____

You were bathed in a big tub at the age of _____

_____

The toy you loved to play with in the tub was _____

_____

After the bath we would always _____

_____

Bath time was always fun time because _____

_____

_____

_____

{ PHOTO HERE }

First Birthday

Just a year since you're here,
So much has changed since then.
Our lives are sweet and so complete,
We'd choose you again and again.

Your first birthday was celebrated by _____

_____

Guests at the celebration were _____

_____

_____

You were really happy about _____

_____

We felt joyful because _____

_____

The birthday gifts you received were _____

_____

_____

Your reaction to your birthday cake and candles was _____

_____

The sweetest memory of this year is _____

_____

_____

{ PHOTO HERE }

You're frightened of _____
_____

When it comes to speaking, you _____
_____

You always mispronounce _____
_____

You seem more grown up because _____
_____

The sweetest memory of this year is _____
_____

Second Birthday

Oh, you little two-year-old,
What mischief you get into.
More or less, there's a mess,
Wherever you have been to.

You're now able to _____

_____

We can't keep you out of _____

_____

You're fascinated by _____

_____

You love to eat _____

_____

You will never eat _____

_____

You go to sleep at _____

_____

The toy you love most is _____

_____

Your favorite story is _____

_____

Your favorite nursery rhyme is _____

_____

{ PHOTO HERE }

We celebrated your birthday by _____

_____

Guests who attended were _____

_____

Your birthday cake was made of _____

_____

The sweetest memory of this year is _____

_____

_____

_____

Third Birthday

Dear little person, you look so big,
How quickly time does fly.
You talk and talk, on and on,
And your favorite word is "why?"

At three you can _____

_____

You love to spend time playing _____

_____

Your favorite story is _____

_____

Your favorite toy is _____

_____

Your favorite nursery rhyme is _____

_____

You love to eat _____

_____

You're good about sharing _____

_____

But you won't share _____

_____

Your best friend is _____

_____

{ PHOTO HERE }

Your favorite song is _____

_____

We laughed so much the time you _____

_____

We celebrated your birthday by _____

_____

Guests were _____

_____

The sweetest memory of this year is _____

_____

_____

_____

Fourth Birthday

I can't believe how many things
You can do alone,
Independent, four years old,
Wow! How you have grown.

At four you can _____

_____

You insist on _____

_____

You will always _____

_____

But you absolutely will not _____

_____

You really love to _____

_____

You go to bed at _____

_____

Your favorite book is _____

_____

Your favorite game is _____

_____

Your favorite toy is _____

_____

{ PHOTO HERE }

We celebrated your birthday by _____

_____

Guests were _____

_____

Your birthday cake was made of _____

_____

The sweetest memory of this year is _____

_____

_____

_____

Fifth Birthday

Five years have gone so quickly,
And we couldn't love you more,
Happiness surrounds you,
You're a child that we adore.

At five years of age you can _____

_____

Special chores you have are _____

_____

You are very good about _____

_____

There's still a tussle getting you to _____

_____

You're very grown up about _____

_____

You're sometimes naughty about _____

_____

You achieve in _____

_____

You're proudest of _____

_____

Your best buddy is _____

{ PHOTO HERE }

School Bells

All dressed up to go to school,
You're the cutest one of all,
I can't believe you're off to class,
You look so very small.

Preschool _____

_____

Located at _____

_____

Teachers _____

_____

_____

_____

Kindergarten _____

_____

Located at _____

_____

Teachers _____

_____

_____

_____

Elementary school _____

_____

Located at _____

_____

Teachers _____

_____

_____

_____

After-school classes _____

_____

_____

Located at _____

_____

_____

Activity _____

_____

_____

Teachers _____

_____

_____

_____

_____

_____

_____

_____

The first time you went to school you _____

_____

_____

You were most interested in _____

_____

_____

Your ambition was _____

_____

_____

Your best school buddy was _____

_____

_____

Your favorite teacher was _____

_____

_____

We beamed when your teacher said _____

_____

_____

_____

_____

_____

_____

_____

{ PHOTO HERE }

Another holiday we shared was _____

_____

Date _____

We celebrated with _____

_____

Traditions of this holiday include _____

_____

_____

Another holiday we shared was _____

_____

Date _____

We celebrated with _____

_____

Traditions of this holiday include _____

_____

_____

Holidays

Holidays are special,
A time we love to share.
It's joy and fun for everyone,
Now that you are here.

The first holiday we celebrated together was _____

_____

Date _____

We celebrated with _____

_____

Traditions of this holiday include _____

_____

_____

_____

Another holiday we shared was _____

_____

Date _____

We celebrated with _____

_____

Traditions of this holiday include _____

_____

_____

_____

Doctor's name _____

_____

Your reaction to the doctor was _____

_____

When it came to shots you _____

_____

Immunization history: _____

DATE   SHOT   TO PROTECT AGAINST

_____

_____

_____

_____

_____

_____

_____

_____

_____

_____

_____

_____

_____

_____

Keeping You Well

We're off to the doctor,
And sometimes there's a tear,
But hugs and kisses always help
To make your smile reappear.

It was clear you weren't feeling well when _____

_____

_____

_____

To comfort you we would _____

_____

_____

_____

Generally your health was _____

_____

_____

_____

It is important for you to know that _____

_____

_____

_____

_____

{ PHOTO HERE }

{ PHOTO HERE }

{ PHOTO HERE }

{ PHOTO HERE }

Growing Up

Eat your vegetables, drink your milk
So you can grow so tall,
You're quickly outgrowing everything,
And you're the sweetest child of all.

	HEIGHT	WEIGHT
Three months		
Six months		
One year		
Eighteen months		
Two years		
Three years		
Four years		
Five years		

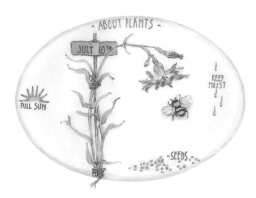

The Middle Years

The years six through twelve
Hurried by so fast,
Elementary school and middle school,
Were soon far in the past.

As a student you were _____
_____
_____
_____

Your favorite subject in school was _____
_____
_____

Your favorite teacher _____
_____
_____
_____

Your best friend _____
_____
_____
_____

For fun you really loved to _____

_____

_____

_____

You never wanted to _____

_____

_____

_____

You had a talent for _____

_____

_____

_____

Your favorite foods were _____

_____

_____

_____

Your room could best be described as _____

_____

_____

_____

What we remember most about those years is _____

_____

_____

_____

The Teenage Years

Suddenly our young child,
Was no longer in sight,
Right before our eyes,
You'd grown up overnight.

The high school you attended _____

_____

_____

You graduated on _____

_____

_____

After high school you planned to _____

_____

_____

_____

Your best friends were _____

_____

_____

In your spare time you liked to _____

_____

_____

_____

Your favorite television programs were _____
_____

_____

Your favorite music groups were _____
_____

_____

As a teenager you once got into hot water for _____
_____

_____

_____

It was difficult to get you to _____
_____

_____

_____

You were especially wonderful about _____
_____

_____

_____

_____

What we remember most about those years is _____
_____

_____

_____

_____

_____

{ PHOTO HERE }

Your Special Day

We looked forward to this day,
With great anticipation.
We love you and we're proud of you,
On your special celebration.

Date _____

_____

We were celebrating your _____

_____

Where _____

_____

We celebrated by _____

_____

_____

Guests who shared this happy occasion were _____

_____

_____

We were so proud of you because _____

_____

_____

_____

The dearest memory of that special day is _____

_____

_____

_____

A Sharing

The years have gone by so swiftly,
Some things may have gone unsaid.
If there's anything you want to know,
Ask whatever pops into your head.

A thought we'd like to share with you is _____

_____

_____

_____

_____

_____

_____

_____

Any choices you ever make we'll support because _____

_____

_____

_____

_____

_____

_____

_____

_____

_____

We'll always be there for you because _____

_____

_____

_____

_____

_____

_____

_____

We've always wanted you to know that _____

_____

_____

_____

_____

_____

_____

_____

We're very proud to be your parents because _____

_____

_____

_____

_____

_____

_____

{ PHOTO HERE }

Looking Ahead

The moment our lives touched,
All our dreams came true,
And the future is a rainbow,
We'll love sharing with you.

Our wishes for your future are _____
_____
_____
_____

When it comes to summing up how we feel about you, always
know that _____
_____
_____
_____
_____
_____
_____

For information, write:
Andrews McMeel Publishing
An Andrews McMeel Universal company
4520 Main Street
Kansas City, Missouri 64111

Produced by Welcome Enterprises, Inc.

ISBN: 0-7407-2709-5

03 04 05 06 WKT 10 9 8 7 6 5 4